Stress Struggles?

Don Barnes

Published by Don Barnes, 2024.

Table of Contents

About the Author

Don is the founder and author of Life Works in Threes!™ E-books. He is a lifelong Texan who has traveled extensively while taking a keen interest in human behavior. His curiosity about life and what drives humans led him to the discovery of how life works in threes. He coined this term as the *Tryune Concept.*

Don attended college on an athletic scholarship and then embarked on a 30-year career in the oil and gas industry. Since the year 2000, he has been a consultant for distributors and manufacturers of various industries. Along the way, he worked on his Tryune discovery in hopes of someday sharing his findings with those struggling unnecessarily... in life. What Don surmised from 40+ years of R&D was that people were struggling unnecessarily because they were not aware that "life works in threes." They, for the most part, have been living their lives <u>by chance</u> rather than <u>by choice,</u> he also discovered.

From this, he began focusing on the "mechanics of life" which shows formulas for success with subjects such as *life, health, money, purpose and so forth.* When people are able to grasp the Tryune Concept, they can apply the formulas with topics that interest them and begin eliminating the struggle. This epiphany is what triggered his Tryune venture and is now on the path of sharing with all who desire to improve on their lives.

Don currently resides in Southern California and Texas while overseeing his businesses and investments.

Life Works in Threes™

When I was a kid growing up, no one sat me down and said, "Okay Don, I'm going to show you how life works so that you can navigate your way through adulthood." I graduated from school, got married and went about my way with the "learn as you go" concept. It was kind of like putting together a backyard swing set without a set of instructions. Lots of frustration and do-overs, for sure!

My discovery of the "triune" word and noticing how things come together in threes is really what set me off on researching that maybe "life comes in three" ...sort of a mechanical approach to managing life, if you will. I combed the libraries and bookstores for information on this and found one book on the subject that was written back in 1951. The author's name was John S. Arant.

What Mr. Arant had to say is this "For lack of a better name, I have called this *The Triangle of Triumph* and therefore, consistent with the name, since most of these conclusions are built on the geometric figure of the triangle." He continued "All Life and all lives are seated in, and circumscribed by, the triangle. The Author and Source and Director of all life is Himself triune in character – Father, Son, and Holy Spirit. Man is of triple nature – body, mind, and spirit – and within those three there are many triangles – desires, development, decay; intellect, will, sensibilities. Of this "paced interlude in the midst of eternity" which we call time there is the triangle of Past, Present, and Future. Space – that limitless and measureless element of the physical universe – is best known in terms of Height, Breadth, and Depth. Try building yourself some triangles along the lines of your Will, your Work, your Way – You will find some interesting angles.

So, for the first time, I realized that life is designed in a mechanical way to come in threes. That means you don't have to rely on wishing and hoping things turn out okay. You can actually look at the three parts that a particular thing is made of and then apply them to get what you're wanting. Like a three-ingredient recipe or a combination lock. With a combination lock, you need the three exact numbers to unlock the lock...otherwise you will continue to struggle.

Some 40 years later, I accumulated things that work in threes and that's when I knew I needed to share this with anyone wanting answers. To have success/harmony in your life, just apply the three parts of an area you're working on, and things will fall into place. I also learned that the recipe for success with just about anything is by doing these three things, consistently – THINK positively, SPEAK positively and ACT positively. For example, if I want to be a successful artist. I would think to myself "I can do this because I have the talent." Then I would speak it this way "Yes, I am working on my art degree and plan to do portraits professionally." Finally, I would act on that by taking art classes and continue crafting my skill. Eventually, I will see the positive results/ success I'm looking for.

Conversely, if I think positively but speak negatively...it will cancel out. Or if I speak positively but have no positive action going on...nothing will happen.

I looked up "How Life Works" and "The Mechanics of Life" and these are really talking about the biology of how our cells work and other chemistry. TRYUNE WORKS! teaches that life is kind of like building blocks. Pick a topic you may be struggling with. See the three parts that topic consists of and then start applying them...on a consistent basis. That will help you overcome the struggle and get you back in harmony/ success with how life works.

For 30+ years I was a golf instructor (by accident). My two kids had some success playing junior golf and so friends and neighbors would ask me to show them and their kids how to play golf successfully. From all of this, I got pretty good at watching golfers on the driving range and could spot right away why they were struggling with hitting bad golf shots. I was able to do that because I knew the three steps to hitting good golf shots. I learned them from studying golf and played for several decades. I "broke the code" for me so to speak.

So now you know that life works in threes. You can live your life *by choice* rather than *by chance* and that my friend... is the key to a fulfilling life.

LIFE WORKS
IN THREES!

My sanctuary on the Pacific coast

Introduction

Managing stress effectively in today's fast-paced world often hinges on a few key strategies:

1. **Self-Awareness**: Recognizing the signs of stress is the first step. This includes paying attention to both physical symptoms (like headaches, fatigue, or changes in appetite) and emotional indicators (such as irritability, anxiety, or mood swings). Regularly check in with yourself to assess how you're feeling and identify any sources of stress. Journaling, mindfulness practices, or even just taking a few moments each day to reflect can help increase self-awareness.

2. **Effective Time Management**: Modern life can be overwhelming with numerous responsibilities and commitments. Developing strong time management skills can help you stay organized and reduce stress. This might involve setting realistic goals, prioritizing tasks, and breaking larger projects into smaller, manageable steps. Utilizing tools like calendars, to-do lists, and reminders can keep you on track and prevent last-minute rushes.

3. **Healthy Coping Mechanisms**: Finding positive ways to cope with stress is crucial. This might include engaging in regular physical activity, practicing relaxation techniques such as deep breathing or meditation, and maintaining a balanced diet. Also, nurturing social connections and seeking support from friends, family, or professionals can provide emotional relief and practical advice. Remember, what works for one person might not work for another, so it's important to explore different coping strategies to find what suits you best.

By focusing on these three areas—self-awareness, time management, and healthy coping—you can better recognize and manage stress in today's world.

My discovery of the Tryune Concept

Before we dive into stress struggles and how to overcome them, let me share my discovery of the Tryune Concept and how life works in threes. It all began in the summer of 1982.

I grew up with parents who treated everyone with decency and respect. My three older sisters and I were raised in a home that was "middle-class traditional." We lived in modest homes in different small towns, attended school and church on a regular basis and celebrated all the traditional holidays. Eventually we settled during the spring of 1964 in the big city of Houston, Texas. I'll never forget the vastness of the city and hearing sirens from police cars, fire trucks and ambulances on a regular basis. I was excited and scared at the same time.

Once settled in this fast-paced city, I finished my growing-up years with an academic diploma and sweetheart intact. I got a job, bought a car, got married, bought a house and produced two beautiful babies in a span of about 5 years. Talk about having to grow up fast!

Things went from great in my childhood to absolute misery in my young adulthood. I began to struggle with my job because deep down I just hated what I was doing. This problem created a snowball effect because soon after, my weight, my finances, my relationships, my happiness and everything else worth saving was going down the drain. I eventually hit a level of frustration that I had never experienced before and didn't know how to get out of it. My cry for help was for anyone or anything to come to my rescue. I just ran out of solutions for my situation.

This is when my discovery happened.

One night shortly after my meltdown, while sleeping soundly, the word "triune" began to softly pound in my head like a mantra. I woke up a little startled and decided to go look up the word in my favorite dictionary (this was WAY before Google.) The definition said '**triune** (try-une) – 1) a group of three things; united. 2) Being 3 in 1 such as *humans are mental, physical and spiritual.* I scratched my head, got a glass of water and went back to bed.

The next day while driving around town, I began thinking about things that I was taught in my younger years that came in threes. My Boy Scout manual taught that to have **character**, I needed to be *1) physically strong,* 2) *mentally awake and 3) morally straight.* My high school football coach would say emphatically "If you want to be **a good football player**, you have to be *1) mobile 2) agile and 3) hostile!*" My first sales manager shared with me that to be **a successful salesman**, I needed to have *1) sales skills, 2) product knowledge and 3) a good image.*

"Hmm", I thought, "wonder if there are other examples out there of things that work in threes?" So, some 40 years later, I have researched and discovered that many, many things work in threes. What this message was telling me is that to achieve success or balance in any significant area of my life, the three things that area consisted of had to be present continuously. That's when I had my epiphany. This discovery was telling me the secret to how life <u>really</u> works.

Tryune is a play on the word "triune" as an invitation to "try" this concept. Furthermore, we do not say that life <u>only</u> works in threes. Life also works in ones, twos, fours and so on. What has been observed though is that the many things significant to life, just so happen to come and work in threes. That's what is being shared in this book.

Now, you are about to see 40+ years of research and proof that life works in threes. I did not make up any of these topics. I invite you to research them on the internet to validate what is written here. There are some interesting facts that most of us have never realized...until now.

How Life Works in Threes (around 200 examples)

<u>**LIFE**</u>

Humans consist of *body, mind and soul.*

A human's basic needs are *health, income and provisions.*

A human's basic wants are *comfort, gain and approval.*

Our minds are made up of the *conscious, the subconscious and the unconscious.*

Philosophy explains *the id, the ego and superego.*

Atoms consist of *protons, neutrons and electrons.*

Motion is explained by *three basic laws.*

Science falls under three main branches: *natural, social and formal sciences*

Time is *past, present and future...*at the same time.

Electricity consists of *ohms, amperes and voltage.*

Music's basic elements are *duration, pitch and timbre.*

Democracy is a government *of the people, by the people and for the people.*

U.S. branches of government are *the judicial, the executive and the legislative.*

Armed Forces protect us on *land, air and sea.*

Environmentally, we are asked *to reduce, recycle and re-use.*

The news program gives us *the news, sports and conditions.*

Our days consist of *morning, afternoon and evening.*

Three months in each season of the year

Our main meals are known as *breakfast, lunch and dinner.*

A balanced diet consists of *good proteins, carbohydrates and fats.*

Traditional Family consists of *father, mother, and child(ren)*

SCIENCES

Three major branches of natural science – *(physical, earth/space and life sciences)*

Three major branches of modern physics - *(classical, relativistic, quantum)*

Three major branches of biology *(botany, zoology, microbiology)*

Three spatial dimensions: *height* (up/down), *width* (left/right) and *depth* (forwards/backwards)

Three-gauge bosons (photon, gluon, W&Z bosons)

Three types of elementary particles *(leptons, quarks, gauge bosons)*

Three quarks in every proton *(two "up" and one "down")*

Three primary colors of light *(red, green, blue)*

Three color tone properties *(hue, value, chroma)*

Three laws of motion *(Newton's laws)*

Three laws of planetary motion *(Kepler's laws)*

Three layers of the Sun's interior *(core, radiative zone, convective zone)*

Three layers of the Sun's atmosphere *(photosphere, chromosphere, corona)*

Three types of meteorites *(iron, stony iron, stony)*

Three types of galaxy shapes *(elliptical, spiral, irregular)*

Three substances of the universe *(normal matter, 'dark matter', 'dark energy')*

Three phases of the moon *(new moon, first quarter, full moon)*

Three planetary regions *(temperate, sub-tropical, tropical)*

Three layers of the Earth *(crust, mantle, core)*

Three components of an ecosystem *(producers, consumers, decomposers)*

Three types of rocks *(igneous, sedimentary, metamorphic)*

Three types of fossil fuels *(coal, crude oil, natural gas)*

Three hydrological processes *(evaporation, condensation, precipitation)*

Three basic types of (meteorological) precipitation *(liquid, freezing, frozen)*

Three types of substances *(mono-constituent, multi-constituent, UVCB)*

Three phases of (normal) matter (*solid, liquid, gas*)

Three types of covalent chemical bonds (*single, double and triple bonds*)

Three isotopes of hydrogen (*protium, deuterium, tritium*)

Three atoms in each molecule of water (*two hydrogen atoms and an oxygen atom*)

Three endings to salts (*-ide, -ite, -ate*)

Three requirements for fire (*fuel, oxygen, heat*)

Three nucleotide bases in a genetic codon

Three domains of life (*archaea, bacteria and eukaryotes*)

Three major groups of flowering plants (*monocots, eudicots, magnolids*)

Three major functions that are basic to plant growth and development: (*photosynthesis* [making sugars], *respiration* [metabolizing those sugars], and *transpiration* [water vapor loss]

Three things that the chlorophyll in plants needs for photosynthesis to take place: (*sunlight, carbon dioxide and water*)

Transpiration serves three roles: (*cooling the plant, moving minerals* and *sugars through the plant,* and *maintaining the turgidity pressure* [stiffness] *of the plant's cells*)

Three parts of an insect's body (*head, thorax, abdomen*)

BIOLOGY

Three types of cones in the retina, relating to the three primary colors

Three semi-circular canals in the ear *(lateral, anterior, posterior)*

Three sections in the ear *(outer, middle, inner)*

Three ossicles in the middle ear *(malleus, incus, stapes)*

Three segments to each limb *(proximal, mid, distal)*

Three bones in each arm *(humerus, radius, ulna)*

Three joints in the arm *(shoulder, elbow, wrist)*

Three joints in the leg *(hip, knee, ankle)*

Three joints in the elbow *(humeroulnar, humeroradial, proximal radioulnar)*

Three functional compartments in the knee joint *(the femoropatellar, medial femorotibial* and *lateral femorotibial articulations)*

Three types of fibrous joints *(sutures, gomphoses, syndesmoses)*

Three types of bone in each hand *(carpals, metacarpals, phalanges)*

Three types of bone in each foot *(tarsals, metatarsals, phalanges)*

Three bones (phalanges) in each finger and in each toe (*proximal, intermediate, distal*)

Three layers of skin (*dermis, epidermis, hypodermis*)

Three components of a cell (*cell membrane, nucleus, cytoplasm*)

Three types of blood vessels (*arteries, veins, capillaries*)

Three types of blood cells [*red* (erythrocytes), *white* (leukocytes), *platelets* (thrombocytes)]

Three processes of the intestinal tract (*ingestion, digestion, excretion*)

Three germ layers (*Endoderm, Mesoderm, Ectoderm*)

Three parts of a human tooth (*crown, neck, root*)

Three organs of otolaryngology (*ear, nose, throat*)

Three major body systems (*digestive, circulatory, respiratory*)

Three parts to a neuron: (*soma* [*cell body*], *axon, dendrites*)

Three main parts of the brain (*forebrain, midbrain, hindbrain*)

Three parts of the forebrain (*cerebrum, thalamus, hypothalamus*)

Three parts of the midbrain (*colliculi, tegmentum, cerebral peduncles*)

Three parts of the hindbrain (*cerebellum, pons, medulla*)

Three membranes enclosing the brain (*dura mater, arachnoid, pia mater*)

The brain operates on three levels: *consciously* (for cognitive thought and declarative memory); *subconsciously* (for pre-planned actions and procedural memory); and *unconsciously* (for breathing, heart beating, etc.)

Our conscious mind is fed from three sources: *our senses* (which can be fooled); *our memory* (which is flawed); and *our imagination* (which is inventive)

Three aspects of the human mind (*memory, intellect, will*)

Three parts of the human personality (*id, ego, superego*)

The sum of human capacity consists of three abilities (*thought, word and deed*)

Three times of man (*birth, life, death*)

Three periods of the Gait Cycle (*initial double limb support, single limb support, and terminal double limb support*)

MUSIC

Three types of musical notes (*sharps, flats, naturals*)

Three aspects of a song (*lyrics, melody, rhythm*)

Three types of musical chords (*root, third, fifth*)

MATHEMATICS

Three types of a real number (*positive, negative, zero*)

Three parts to any arithmetic operation: for addition: *augend, addend and sum* - for subtraction: *minuend, subtrahend and difference* - for multiplication: *multiplicand, multiplier and product* - for division: *dividend, divisor and quotient*

Three laws of arithmetic operations (*commutative, associative, distributive*)

Three types of equivalence relation (*reflexivity, symmetry, transitivity*)

Three types of symmetry operations (*translation, rotation, reflection*)

Three geometries (*Euclidean, spherical, hyperbolic*)

The number 3 is the basis of an entire branch of mathematics, called trigonometry (from the Greek *trigonon* "triangle" + *metron* "measure")

Three trigonometric functions (*sine, cosine, tangent*)

Three types of average (*mean, mode, median*)

GRAMMAR

Three logical operators (*AND, OR and NOT*)

Three laws of logic (*identity, noncontradiction, excluded middle*)

Three parts of a logical syllogism (*major premise, minor premise, conclusion*)

Three grammatical parts to a sentence (*subject, verb, complement*)

Three persons in grammar [*1st person* (I/we), *2nd* (you or your), *3rd* (he/she/it/they)]

Three genders in grammar [*masculine* (he/him), *feminine* (she/her), *neuter* (it)]

Three forms of comparison in grammar [*positive, comparative* (more, -er), *superlative* (most, -est)]

Three cases in (English) grammar [*subjective/nominative* (he), *objective/accusative* (him) and *possessive/genitive* (his)]

Three parts of a narrative (*beginning, middle, end*)

Components of an essay (*introduction, body, conclusion*)

Elements of a rhetorical appeal (*ethos, pathos, logos*)

Aspects of a story (*plot, characters, setting*)

<u>RELIGION</u>

The Creator – *omniscient, omnipotent, omnipresent*

Christian God – *Father, Son, Holy Spirit*

Jesus – *The Way, The Truth, The Life*

Ancient Near East- *Qudshu, Astarte, Anat*

Classical Antiquity – Many dieties came in threes

Hinduism – Para Brahman is *Brahma, Visnu, Shiva*

Ancient Celtic Cultures – *many example of triad dieties*

Buddhism – *The three jewels*

Taoism – *The three pure ones*

Islam – *Fear, Hope and Love*

Baha'i - *Intention, Power and Action*

Confucianism – *Benevolence, Wisdom and Courage*

OTHER TRIUNE EXAMPLES

3 Coins in a Fountain

3 Days of the Condor

3 Miles in a League

3 Goals in a Hat Trick

3 Piece Suit

3 Feet in a Yard

3 Books in Lord of the Rings

3 Ring Circus

3 Ships of Christopher Columbus

3 Sheets to the Wind

3 Books in a Trilogy

3 Wheels on a Tricycle

3 Wise Men

3-Legged Race

3 Ring Circus

3-Wheeler

3 Cornered Hat

3 Dimensional

3 Musketeers

3 R's (reading, 'riting, 'rithmatic)

3 Sides of a triangle

3 Races in the Triple Crown (horse racing)

3 Angles in a Triangle

3 Trimesters in a Pregnancy

3 Flavors in Neapolitan Ice Cream

3 Stars in Orion's belt

3 Barleycorns in an Inch

3 Hands on a Clock (with the Seconds Hand)

3 Colors in a Flag

3 Minute Egg

3 Great Pyramids at Giza

3 Holes in a Bowling Ball

3 Colors in a Set of Traffic Lights

3 Minutes in a Boxing Round

3 Teaspoons in a Tablespoon

3 Legs on a Stool

3 Monastic Vows (Obience, Stability, Conversatio Morum)

3 Body Types: Endomorph, Mesomorph, Ectomorph

3 Ring Notebooks

3 Germ layers: Endoderm, Mesoderm, Ectoderm

3 Species of Homo: Homo habilis, Homo erectus, Homo sapiens

3 Basic parts of a camera: Lens, Shutter, Sensor

3 Stages of a Project lifecycle: initiation, planning, execution

The Truth, The Whole Truth and Nothing but the Truth

Life, Liberty and the Pursuit of Happiness

Hear no Evil, See no Evil, Speak no Evil

National motto of France/Haiti: Liberty, Equality, Fraternity

Paper, Rock, Scissors

Ready, Aim, Fire

On Your mark, Get Set, Go

Olympic medals of gold, silver, bronze

Types of joints (ball & socket, hinge, pivot)

Stages of a rocket launch (launch, orbit, re-entry)

Parts of a joke (setup, delivery, punchline)

Primary components of a transistor (emitter, base, collector)

Primary components of an airplane (fuselage, wings, empennage)

Basic components of a computer: CPU, memory, storage

Three phases in the development of technology (*eotechnic* [*mechanical*], *paleotechnic* [*steam-powered*] and *neotechnic* [*electric-powered*]

Communication systems require three components (*transmitter, channel, receiver*)

The list goes on. See if you can find more examples as they are everywhere in our universe! Now that you know that life works in threes (with proof!), we can begin to apply this concept to whatever topics we want.

So, to overcome struggles with stress, we need to apply the three areas that stress consists of – RECOGNIZE, TIME MANAGING and COPING SKILLS. Let's get started!

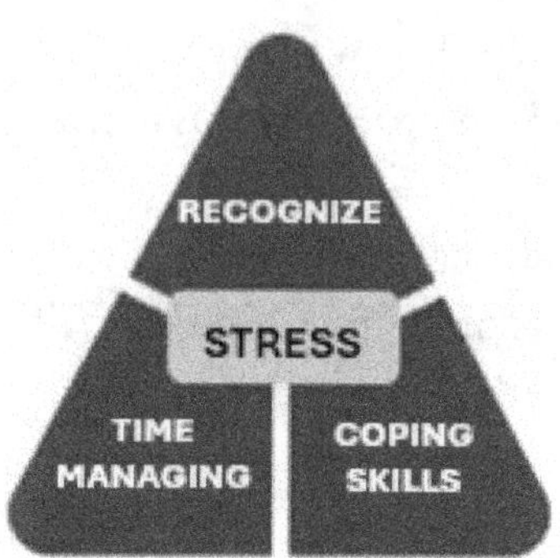

RECOGNIZE
STRESS
TIME
MANAGING
COPING
SKILLS

STRESS

Stress can manifest in various forms, and understanding the different types can help you manage and address them more effectively. Here's a list of some common kinds of stress that people experience:

1. **Acute Stress**: This is short-term stress that arises from immediate challenges or pressures. It's often intense but usually resolves quickly once the situation is over. For example, stress from meeting a deadline or a sudden argument.

2. **Chronic Stress**: This type of stress persists over a long period, often due to ongoing life situations or problems. It can result from continuous pressures such as long-term financial difficulties, job dissatisfaction, or unresolved relationship issues.

3. **Eustress**: This is positive stress that can motivate and energize you. It often arises from situations that are exciting or challenging, such as starting a new job, planning a wedding, or taking on a new project. Eustress is generally perceived as manageable and can enhance performance.

4. **Distress**: This is negative stress that can be overwhelming and detrimental to your well-being. It often stems from situations perceived as threats or challenges that exceed your ability to cope, such as serious illness, financial problems, or a traumatic event.

5. **Episodic Acute Stress**: This form of stress occurs in episodes or bursts. It is similar to acute stress but happens frequently. Individuals with episodic acute stress may experience recurring issues like frequent arguments, persistent job pressure, or ongoing personal conflicts.

6. **Traumatic Stress**: This stress results from experiencing or witnessing traumatic events such as accidents, natural disasters,

or violent incidents. It can lead to conditions like Post-Traumatic Stress Disorder (PTSD) and may require professional intervention to manage effectively.

7. **Environmental Stress**: This type comes from external factors in your surroundings, such as noise, pollution, or crowded living conditions. It can affect your health and well-being over time.

8. **Social Stress**: Stress arising from social interactions or relationships, including conflicts with friends, family dynamics, or difficulties in social settings. Social stress can impact your emotional state and social functioning.

9. **Work-Related Stress**: This includes stressors related to the workplace, such as job insecurity, excessive workload, long hours, conflicts with colleagues, or lack of control over job responsibilities.

10. **Health-Related Stress**: Stress related to physical health issues, whether it's managing a chronic illness, dealing with a sudden health scare, or the stress of maintaining a healthy lifestyle.

11. **Academic Stress**: This type affects students and learners, stemming from pressures related to exams, coursework, grades, and academic performance.

12. **Financial Stress**: Stress related to financial concerns, including managing debt, budgeting, saving, and the overall economic instability that can affect personal finances.

Understanding these different types of stress can help you identify what might be affecting you and take appropriate steps to address each type effectively.

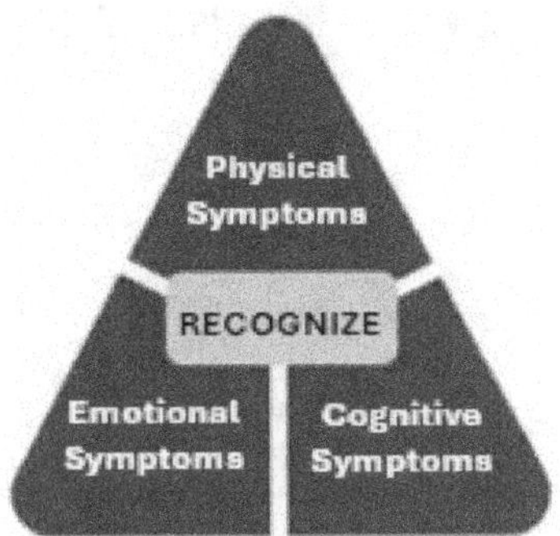
Physical
Symptoms
RECOGNIZE
Emotional
Symptoms
Cognitive
Symptoms

RECOGNIZE

Recognizing stress involves paying attention to various signs and symptoms that might indicate someone is struggling. Here are three key ways to identify stress:

1. **Physical Symptoms**: Stress often manifests through physical changes in the body. Common physical signs include headaches, muscle tension, fatigue, digestive issues, and sleep disturbances (such as insomnia or excessive sleeping). Frequent illness or weakened immune response can also be indicators. If someone is experiencing persistent physical symptoms without a clear medical cause, stress might be a contributing factor.

2. **Emotional and Behavioral Changes**: Emotional symptoms of stress can include irritability, anxiety, depression, mood swings, and feeling overwhelmed. Behavioral changes might involve withdrawal from social activities, increased reliance on unhealthy coping mechanisms (like alcohol or drugs), or changes in eating habits. Noticeable shifts in how someone interacts with others or their general demeanor can signal stress.

3. **Cognitive and Mental Symptoms**: Stress can affect cognitive functions and mental clarity. Signs to look for include difficulty concentrating, memory problems, indecisiveness, or a constant feeling of being overwhelmed by tasks. If someone is struggling to focus on work or daily responsibilities or is frequently preoccupied with worries, it could indicate high levels of stress.

By paying attention to these physical, emotional, and cognitive signs, you can better recognize when someone may be experiencing stress and offer support or encourage them to seek professional help if needed.

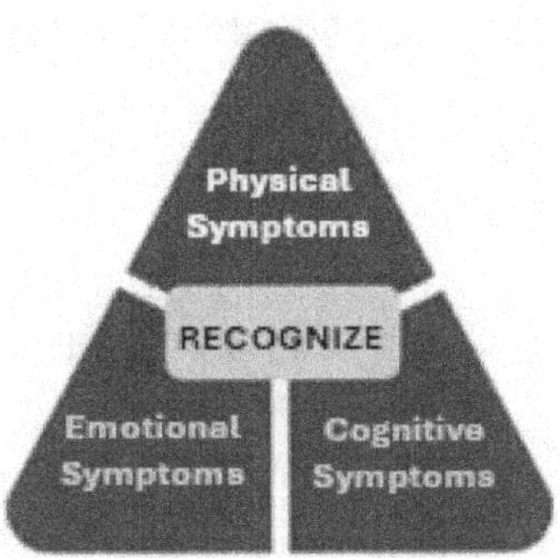
Physical
Symptoms
RECOGNIZE
Emotional
Symptoms
Cognitive
Symptoms

Physical Symptoms

Physical symptoms of stress can vary widely but often manifest in the following ways:

1. **Headaches:** Tension headaches or migraines are common stress-related symptoms.
2. **Muscle Tension:** Stiffness or pain in the neck, shoulders, and back, as well as general muscle aches.
3. **Fatigue:** Persistent tiredness or exhaustion, even after adequate rest.
4. **Digestive Issues:** Problems such as stomachaches, nausea, diarrhea, constipation, or changes in appetite.
5. **Sleep Disturbances:** Difficulty falling asleep, staying asleep, or experiencing restless and unrefreshing sleep.
6. **Chest Pain:** Tightness, pressure, or discomfort in the chest, which can sometimes mimic heart problems.
7. **Rapid Heartbeat:** Palpitations or an increased heart rate, often accompanied by a feeling of anxiety.
8. **Sweating:** Excessive sweating, particularly in stressful situations.
9. **Tremors or Shaking:** Unexplained trembling or shaking of the hands or other parts of the body.
10. **Frequent Illness:** A weakened immune system leading to frequent colds, infections, or other illnesses.
11. **Shortness of Breath:** Difficulty breathing or a sensation of being unable to catch your breath.
12. **Skin Problems:** Breakouts, rashes, or eczema flares that are exacerbated by stress.
13. **Dizziness:** Feeling lightheaded, dizzy, or unsteady, which can be related to stress or anxiety.
14. **Changes in Weight:** Significant weight loss or gain due to

changes in eating habits or metabolism.

15. **Jaw Pain or Clenching**: Pain in the jaw or grinding of teeth, often occurring during sleep or stressful situations.

These physical symptoms can be a response to stress and may vary from person to person. If someone is experiencing these symptoms persistently, it's important to consider stress as a potential factor and seek appropriate support or medical advice.

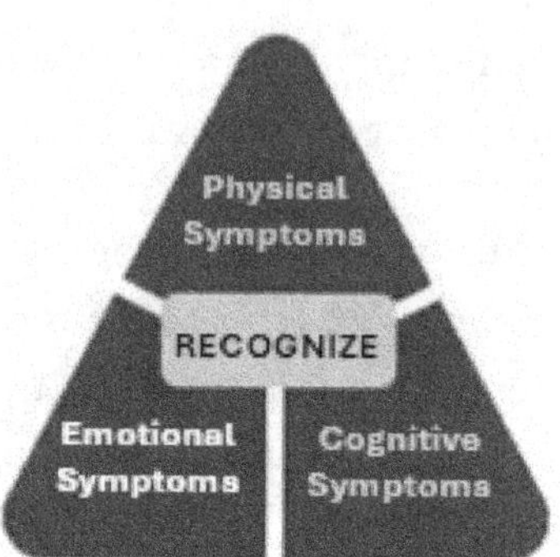
Physical
Symptoms
RECOGNIZE
Emotional
Symptoms
Cognitive
Symptoms

Emotional Symptoms

Emotional symptoms of stress can significantly impact a person's mental well-being and overall mood. Here's a list of common emotional symptoms that may arise during periods of stress:

1. **Anxiety**: Persistent feelings of worry, nervousness, or apprehension about current or future events.
2. **Irritability**: Increased sensitivity, frustration, or anger over minor issues or daily challenges.
3. **Depression**: Feelings of sadness, hopelessness, or a general loss of interest or pleasure in activities once enjoyed.
4. **Overwhelm**: A sense of being unable to cope with the demands and pressures of daily life.
5. **Mood Swings**: Rapid and unpredictable changes in emotional states, from feeling fine to suddenly being upset or angry.
6. **Restlessness**: An inability to relax or a constant feeling of being on edge.
7. **Low Self-Esteem**: Reduced confidence or self-worth, often accompanied by negative self-talk or self-doubt.
8. **Difficulty Concentrating**: Trouble focusing on tasks or making decisions, leading to feelings of frustration or incompetence.
9. **Feelings of Isolation**: A sense of loneliness or detachment from others, even when surrounded by people.
10. **Panic Attacks**: Sudden episodes of intense fear or discomfort, often accompanied by physical symptoms like a racing heart or shortness of breath.
11. **Emotional Numbness**: A feeling of being emotionally disconnected or numb, as if unable to fully experience emotions.
12. **Increased Sensitivity**: Heightened emotional responses to

situations that might not normally provoke a strong reaction.

13. **Guilt or Shame**: Feeling guilty or ashamed about not meeting expectations or about one's own stress response.

14. **Indifference or Apathy**: A lack of enthusiasm or motivation to engage in activities or responsibilities, often due to feeling overwhelmed.

15. **Difficulty Managing Emotions**: Struggling to regulate or control emotions, leading to outbursts or difficulty handling stressors calmly.

These emotional symptoms can interfere with daily functioning and relationships, making it crucial to address them through self-care, support systems, or professional help if needed. Recognizing these symptoms is an important step toward managing stress effectively.

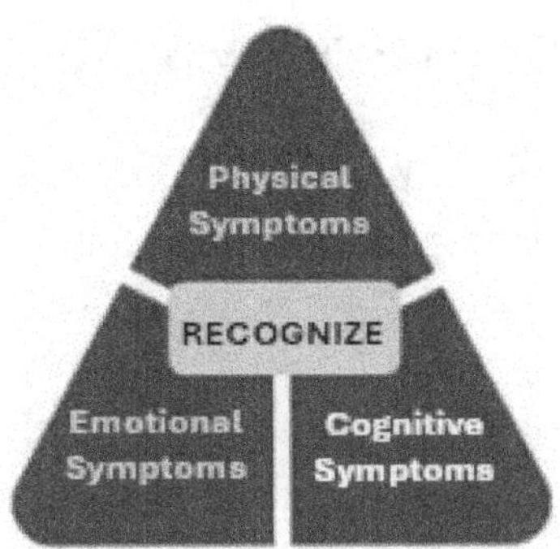
Physical
Symptoms
RECOGNIZE
Emotional
Symptoms
Cognitive
Symptoms

Cognitive Symptoms

Stress can impact cognitive functions in various ways. Here's a list of cognitive symptoms that a person might experience while dealing with stress:

1. **Difficulty Concentrating**: Trouble focusing on tasks or staying engaged in activities, often leading to incomplete work or errors.
2. **Memory Problems**: Issues with short-term or long-term memory, including forgetfulness or difficulty recalling information.
3. **Indecisiveness**: Difficulty making decisions or feeling overwhelmed by choices, leading to procrastination or second-guessing.
4. **Confusion**: A sense of disorientation or mental fog, making it hard to think clearly or process information effectively.
5. **Reduced Cognitive Speed**: Slower thinking, processing, or reaction times, impacting the ability to respond quickly to situations.
6. **Overthinking**: Ruminating excessively on problems or scenarios, often leading to a cycle of worry and anxiety.
7. **Difficulty Planning**: Trouble organizing tasks or setting priorities, which can impact productivity and goal-setting.
8. **Trouble with Problem-Solving**: Reduced ability to come up with solutions to problems or handle complex situations effectively.
9. **Increased Distractibility**: Difficulty maintaining attention on a single task, with frequent distractions or interruptions in focus.
10. **Poor Judgment**: Making decisions that are out of character or not well thought out, often due to impaired clarity or

reasoning.

11. **Mental Fatigue**: Feeling mentally drained or exhausted, leading to decreased cognitive performance and motivation.

12. **Diminished Creativity**: Reduced ability to think creatively or generate new ideas, which can affect problem-solving and innovation.

13. **Difficulty Learning**: Challenges in absorbing new information or learning new skills, often due to cognitive overload or stress-induced distraction.

14. **Disorganization**: Trouble keeping track of tasks, deadlines, or personal belongings, resulting in a disorganized approach to daily life.

15. **Increased Errors**: More frequent mistakes or lapses in judgment, often due to impaired attention or cognitive function under stress.

These cognitive symptoms can affect various aspects of daily life and work, making it important to manage stress effectively and seek support if these symptoms become overwhelming or persistent.

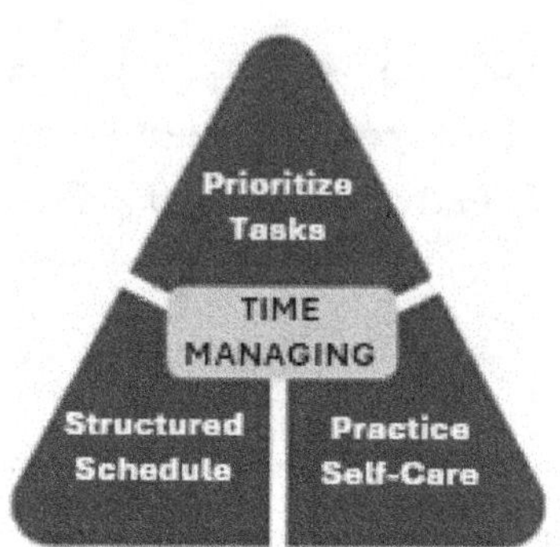
Prioritize
Tasks
TIME
MANAGING
Structured
Schedule
Practice
Self-Care

TIME MANAGING

Managing time effectively while dealing with stress is crucial for maintaining productivity and well-being. Here are three key strategies to help:

Prioritize Tasks:

Identify Key Priorities: Focus on the most important and urgent tasks first. Use tools like the Eisenhower Matrix to categorize tasks into four quadrants: urgent and important, important but not urgent, urgent but not important, and neither urgent nor important. This helps you tackle high-priority items and delegate or defer less critical tasks.

Set Realistic Goals: Break larger tasks into smaller, manageable steps and set achievable deadlines. This prevents feeling overwhelmed and makes it easier to track progress.

Create a Structured Schedule:

Use Time Management Tools: Utilize planners, calendars, or digital tools like apps to organize your schedule. Allocate specific times for work, breaks, and personal activities to maintain a balanced routine.

Implement Time Blocking: Dedicate specific blocks of time to focused work and use separate blocks for breaks and personal time. For example, work in focused intervals (e.g., 25 minutes) followed by short breaks (e.g., 5 minutes) using techniques like the Pomodoro Technique. This helps maintain productivity while managing stress.

Practice Self-Care and Flexibility:

Incorporate Breaks and Downtime: Schedule regular breaks throughout your day to relax and recharge. Short breaks help prevent burnout and maintain mental clarity.

Be Flexible and Adjust: Recognize that unexpected events or higher stress levels may require adjustments to your schedule. Be prepared to shift priorities and modify deadlines as needed. Flexibility helps reduce stress associated with rigid plans and unexpected challenges.

By focusing on prioritizing tasks, creating a structured schedule, and practicing self-care with flexibility, you can manage your time more effectively even when dealing with stress.

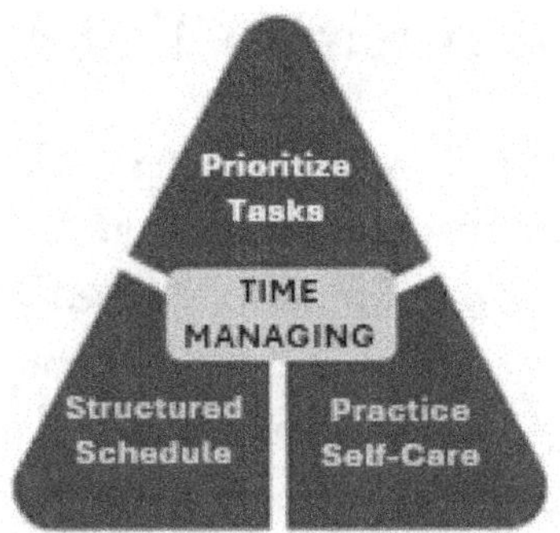
Prioritize
Tasks
TIME
MANAGING
Structured
Schedule
Practice
Self-Care

Prioritize Tasks

Prioritizing tasks effectively while dealing with stress is essential for maintaining both productivity and mental well-being. Start by identifying and categorizing your tasks based on their urgency and importance. This can be achieved using methods like the Eisenhower Matrix, which divides tasks into four categories: urgent and important, important but not urgent, urgent but not important, and neither urgent nor important. By focusing on tasks that are both urgent and important first, you can address immediate needs and avoid the pressure of looming deadlines. Prioritizing helps ensure that your most critical responsibilities are managed, reducing feelings of overwhelm and allowing for a clearer focus on what truly matters.

Once you've categorized your tasks, break them down into smaller, more manageable steps. Large projects can often feel daunting, especially when under stress, leading to procrastination or feelings of being overwhelmed. By dividing these tasks into smaller, actionable components, you make progress feel more achievable and less intimidating. Set realistic deadlines for each step and celebrate small victories along the way. This approach not only helps in managing stress but also boosts motivation by providing a sense of accomplishment as you complete each part of the task.

In addition to breaking down tasks, it's important to incorporate flexibility into your prioritization process. Stressful situations often come with unexpected challenges and changes, so rigidity in your planning can lead to increased anxiety. Be prepared to reassess and adjust your priorities as needed. If new tasks arise or deadlines shift, adapt your plan accordingly and communicate with relevant stakeholders if necessary. By remaining flexible and adjusting your priorities based on evolving circumstances, you can better manage stress and maintain control over your workload.

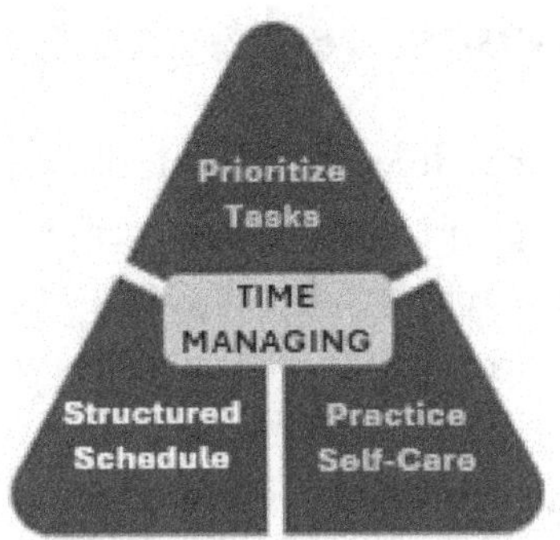

Prioritize
Tasks
TIME
MANAGING
Structured
Schedule
Practice
Self-Care

Structured Schedule

Creating a structured schedule is crucial for coping with stress because it provides a clear framework for managing time and responsibilities. A well-organized schedule helps to break down overwhelming tasks into smaller, manageable parts, which can significantly reduce anxiety. By allocating specific times for work, breaks, and personal activities, you establish a routine that can bring a sense of order and predictability to your day. This structured approach ensures that you stay focused on your priorities, minimizes the likelihood of forgetting important tasks, and prevents last-minute rushes that can heighten stress levels.

Furthermore, a structured schedule promotes balance by incorporating regular intervals for relaxation and self-care. When dealing with stress, it's easy to become consumed by work or obligations, neglecting essential downtime. By intentionally scheduling breaks, leisure activities, and time for self-care, you create a balanced routine that supports both mental and physical health. These scheduled breaks allow you to recharge and return to tasks with renewed energy, ultimately improving productivity and reducing the risk of burnout.

Finally, having a structured schedule enhances your ability to adapt to changes and manage unexpected stressors. When you have a clear plan in place, it becomes easier to identify and address disruptions without losing track of your overall goals. If new tasks or emergencies arise, you can adjust your schedule with greater ease, reallocating time as needed while maintaining a sense of control. This flexibility within a structured framework helps mitigate the impact of stress and enables you to respond to challenges more effectively, fostering resilience and a proactive approach to managing stress.

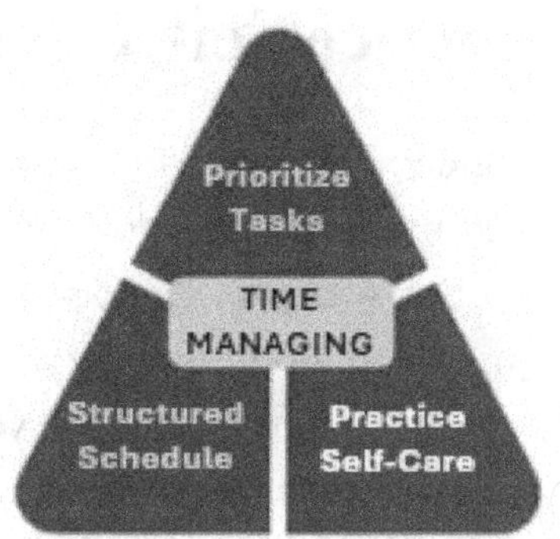
Prioritize
Tasks
TIME
MANAGING
Structured
Schedule
Practice
Self-Care

Practice Self-Care

Practicing self-care is a fundamental aspect of managing stress effectively, as it directly impacts both physical and emotional well-being. Engaging in regular self-care activities—such as exercise, adequate sleep, and a balanced diet—helps maintain your body's resilience against stress. Physical health is closely linked to how well you handle stress; for example, regular physical activity releases endorphins, which act as natural mood lifters and stress reducers. Similarly, sufficient sleep and a nutritious diet contribute to overall health, allowing you to better cope with stress and recover from daily challenges.

Emotional self-care is equally important in managing stress. This involves taking time to engage in activities that bring joy, relaxation, and fulfillment. Pursuing hobbies, practicing mindfulness or meditation, and nurturing relationships with supportive friends and family can significantly alleviate stress and improve emotional stability. By setting aside time for activities that you find personally meaningful and enjoyable, you create a buffer against the pressures of daily life, helping to restore emotional balance and prevent burnout.

Incorporating self-care into your routine also means setting healthy boundaries and recognizing when to seek professional support. It's essential to understand your limits and avoid overcommitting, as taking on too much can exacerbate stress. Learning to say no, delegating tasks, and asking for help when needed are important aspects of self-care. Additionally, seeking support from a mental health professional can provide valuable strategies and tools for managing stress more effectively. By prioritizing self-care and understanding its role in stress management, you enhance your overall resilience and well-being, making it easier to navigate life's challenges.

Relax
COPING
SKILLS
Physical
Activity
Social
Support

COPING SKILLS

Here are three effective coping skills for managing stress:

1. **Mindfulness and Relaxation Techniques**: Practicing mindfulness and relaxation techniques can help manage stress by promoting a sense of calm and improving emotional regulation. Mindfulness involves paying attention to the present moment without judgment, which can reduce anxiety and help you stay grounded. Techniques such as deep breathing exercises, progressive muscle relaxation, and meditation can help lower stress levels by calming the nervous system and providing a mental break from stressors. Incorporating these practices into your daily routine, even for just a few minutes each day, can make a significant difference in your ability to manage stress effectively.

2. **Physical Activity**: Engaging in regular physical activity is a powerful way to cope with stress. Exercise has been shown to boost mood by increasing the production of endorphins, the body's natural stress relievers. Activities like walking, jogging, yoga, or even dancing can help reduce symptoms of stress and anxiety while improving overall physical health. Exercise also provides a constructive outlet for pent-up energy and frustration, helping you feel more relaxed and better equipped to handle stress. Finding an activity you enjoy can make it easier to stick with a regular exercise routine.

3. **Building and Maintaining Social Connections**: Social support is a critical component of stress management. Talking with friends, family, or support groups can provide emotional relief and practical advice. Sharing your feelings with others can help you feel understood and less isolated, and receiving support can offer new perspectives and solutions to stressors.

Engaging in social activities and nurturing relationships can also provide a sense of belonging and connection, which can buffer against stress. Make an effort to stay connected with those who offer positivity and encouragement, and don't hesitate to seek out professional support if needed.

By incorporating these coping skills into your life, you can build resilience and effectively manage stress, leading to improved mental and physical well-being.

Relax
COPING
SKILLS
Physical
Activity
Social
Support

Relax

Relaxation techniques are highly effective tools for managing stress, as they help calm the mind and body, reduce anxiety, and improve overall well-being. One popular method is deep breathing exercises, which involve focusing on slow, deliberate breaths to activate the body's relaxation response. By practicing deep breathing, you engage the parasympathetic nervous system, which counteracts the body's stress response and promotes a state of calm. Techniques such as diaphragmatic breathing, where you breathe deeply into your abdomen rather than shallowly into your chest, can help reduce feelings of tension and provide immediate relief from stress.

Another valuable relaxation technique is progressive muscle relaxation (PMR). This method involves systematically tensing and then relaxing different muscle groups in the body, starting from the toes and working up to the head. By focusing on the contrast between tension and relaxation, PMR helps to release physical stress and improve awareness of muscle tension. This technique can be particularly useful for individuals experiencing stress-related muscle tightness or chronic pain, as it promotes both physical and mental relaxation and enhances overall body awareness.

Mindfulness meditation is also an effective relaxation technique for managing stress. Mindfulness involves paying attention to the present moment with acceptance and without judgment. Through mindfulness meditation, individuals can learn to observe their thoughts and feelings without becoming overwhelmed by them. Regular practice can improve emotional regulation, reduce symptoms of anxiety and depression, and enhance overall mental clarity. Incorporating mindfulness practices into your daily routine, even for a few minutes a day, can foster a sense of inner peace and resilience against stress, making it easier to handle daily challenges with greater ease.

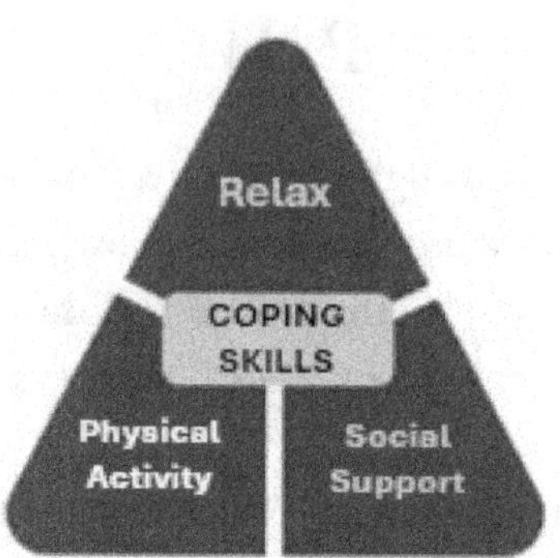
Relax
COPING
SKILLS
Physical
Activity
Social
Support

Physical Activity

Engaging in physical activities is a highly effective way to cope with stress, as it helps reduce the physiological and psychological impacts of stress. One of the most accessible and beneficial forms of exercise is aerobic activity, such as brisk walking, jogging, or cycling. These activities elevate the heart rate and trigger the release of endorphins, which are natural mood lifters. Regular aerobic exercise not only enhances physical fitness but also helps in reducing levels of cortisol, the body's primary stress hormone. Incorporating just 30 minutes of aerobic exercise most days of the week can significantly improve mood and overall stress resilience.

Strength training exercises, such as weightlifting or resistance training, also offer valuable stress-relief benefits. While often associated with building muscle and strength, these activities can provide mental health advantages as well. Engaging in strength training can help channel stress into physical exertion, promoting a sense of accomplishment and control. The structured nature of strength training routines can also create a sense of discipline and focus, which helps counteract feelings of overwhelm. Additionally, the physiological stress of lifting weights triggers the release of endorphins, similar to aerobic exercise, contributing to reduced stress levels and improved mood.

Yoga and stretching exercises offer a unique combination of physical and mental benefits that are particularly effective for stress management. Yoga integrates physical postures, breathing exercises, and mindfulness, creating a holistic approach to stress relief. The practice of yoga encourages relaxation, flexibility, and balance, both physically and mentally. Through mindful movement and deep breathing, yoga helps calm the nervous system and promotes a sense of inner peace. Stretching exercises, while often simpler, can also alleviate physical tension and improve overall relaxation. Incorporating yoga or stretching into your routine can provide a soothing break from daily stressors and enhance overall well-being.

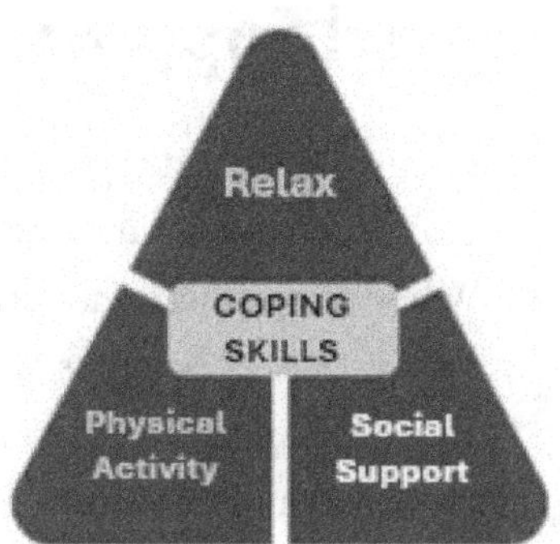

Relax
COPING
SKILLS
Physical
Activity
Social
Support

Social Support

Social support plays a critical role in managing stress, providing both emotional and practical assistance that can significantly alleviate the burden of difficult times. When individuals face stress, having a network of supportive friends, family, or colleagues can offer a sense of connection and understanding. Sharing experiences and emotions with others who listen empathetically can validate feelings and reduce feelings of isolation. This emotional support helps in buffering against the adverse effects of stress and can offer a sense of relief and comfort during challenging periods.

In addition to emotional support, social connections can provide practical help and problem-solving resources. Friends and family often offer advice, assistance, or even just a different perspective on the stressors one is facing. This support can be invaluable in helping to manage daily responsibilities, make informed decisions, and tackle problems more effectively. Whether it's through helping with tasks, offering practical solutions, or simply providing encouragement, having a support network can make stressful situations more manageable and less overwhelming.

Moreover, social support contributes to overall mental health and resilience. Engaging in social activities and maintaining relationships can foster a sense of belonging and community, which is crucial for psychological well-being. Positive interactions with others can elevate mood, provide distraction from stressors, and reinforce a sense of stability. Additionally, the act of supporting others in return can create a reciprocal sense of purpose and fulfillment, further enhancing emotional resilience. In summary, having a robust support system is essential for navigating stressful times, as it offers both emotional comfort and practical aid, ultimately contributing to better mental and physical health.

SUMMARY

Good stress, often referred to as "eustress," is the type of stress that is positive and motivating. It arises from situations that are perceived as challenges or opportunities for growth rather than threats. Examples of good stress include preparing for a new job, taking on a challenging project, or participating in a competitive event. Eustress can enhance performance, increase focus, and provide a sense of excitement and accomplishment. This type of stress generally leads to feelings of satisfaction and a boost in confidence, as it helps individuals push their limits and achieve their goals.

In contrast, bad stress, known as "distress," is negative and overwhelming, often resulting from situations perceived as threats or insurmountable challenges. Distress can arise from chronic issues such as financial problems, job insecurity, or personal conflicts. Unlike eustress, distress typically leads to feelings of anxiety, helplessness, and frustration. It can negatively impact mental and physical health, causing symptoms like fatigue, irritability, and depression. Chronic distress can also lead to burnout and reduced quality of life, as it undermines one's ability to cope effectively with daily demands.

The primary difference between good stress and bad stress lies in their impact on well-being and their outcomes. Good stress is manageable and often leads to personal growth, increased resilience, and a sense of achievement. It motivates individuals to tackle challenges and improve their skills. On the other hand, bad stress overwhelms and diminishes one's capacity to cope, leading to negative health effects and decreased overall functioning. Recognizing the nature of the stress one is experiencing and differentiating between eustress and distress can help in adopting appropriate strategies to manage stress effectively and maintain a healthy balance.

Invitation

Making health a top priority by managing stress is crucial for overall well-being, as stress significantly impacts both physical and mental health. Chronic stress can lead to a range of health issues, including cardiovascular problems, weakened immune function, and digestive disturbances. By actively managing stress through healthy coping strategies, individuals can mitigate these adverse effects and maintain better physical health. Prioritizing health involves not only addressing the direct consequences of stress but also adopting a proactive approach to wellness, which includes regular exercise, a balanced diet, and sufficient sleep.

Mental health is equally affected by stress, and prioritizing health means addressing emotional and psychological well-being. Chronic stress can contribute to mental health issues such as anxiety, depression, and cognitive impairments. By making stress management a priority, individuals can reduce the risk of developing these conditions and enhance their emotional resilience. Techniques such as mindfulness, relaxation exercises, and seeking social support are effective in managing stress and improving mental health. Prioritizing mental health through stress management also supports better decision-making, improved relationships, and a more positive outlook on life.

Additionally, making health a number one priority through effective stress management can lead to a more balanced and fulfilling life. When stress is managed effectively, individuals experience greater energy levels, improved focus, and enhanced productivity. This holistic approach to health not only prevents the negative impacts of stress but also fosters a more harmonious and enjoyable life. By integrating stress management practices into daily routines and prioritizing self-care, individuals can achieve a healthier balance between work, personal life, and overall well-being, ultimately leading to a higher quality of life and greater satisfaction.

When you're with someone who is sharing their struggles with you...just smile at him/her and give them one of these. He/she will ask "What is that?" Then simply reply "Life Works in Threes."

Other titles coming out:

- Weight Struggles?
- Abundance Struggles?
- Parenting Struggles?
- Life Struggles?
- Purpose Struggles?
- Happiness Struggles?
- Sales Struggles?
- Speaker Struggles?
- Time Struggles?
- Network Struggles?
- Marriage Struggles?
- Divorce Struggles?
- Money Struggles?
- Career Struggles?
- Dating Struggles?
- Caretaker Struggles?
- Forgiveness Struggles?
- Grieving Struggles?
- Success Struggles?
- Golf Struggles?
- Workplace Struggles?
- Romance Struggles?
- Shame/Guilt Struggles?
- Addiction Struggles?

Quotes about Stress

"It's not stress that kills us; it is our reaction to it." — Hans Selye

"The greatest weapon against stress is our ability to choose one thought over another." — William James

"Stress is caused by being 'here' but wanting to be 'there,' or being 'now' but wanting to be 'then.'" — Eckhart Tolle

"Stress is like a rocking chair. It gives you something to do but gets you nowhere." — Anonymous

"The time to relax is when you don't have time for it." — Sydney J. Harris

"Adopting the right attitude can convert a negative stress into a positive one." — Hans Selye

"In the midst of chaos, there is also opportunity." — Sun Tzu

"It's not the load that breaks you down, it's the way you carry it." — Lou Holtz

"One of the symptoms of an approaching nervous breakdown is the belief that one's work is terribly important." — Bertrand Russell

"You don't have to control your thoughts. You just have to stop letting them control you." — Dan Millman

Remember,
When you get right down to it,
Life is about making choices.
Every day, all day long, that's what we do.

- *We choose to get out of bed or not.*
- *We choose to clean up or not.*
- *We choose what to eat all day.*
- *We choose to exercise or not.*
- *We choose to go to work or not.*
- *We choose to do a good job or not.*
- *We choose to come home or not.*
- *We choose to watch TV or do something constructive.*
- *We choose to bed at a decent hour or not.*

And the next day...we start all over again.
What is the meaning of this? Get good at choosing.
Before you can get good at choosing though...you need to understand how
life works in threes.

When someone is struggling with a particular area or two, chances are they are "out of balance" with how life works. How does life work? Life works in threes.

If you're interested in personal topics like life, health, money or business topics like sales, time management and public speaking...Life Works in Threes! can shed some light on creating success in those areas.

The definition of TRIUNE is a group of three things; united. Being three in one, such as - humans are *mental, physical* and *spiritual beings.* The word TRYUNE is a play of the word TRIUNE, encouraging all to try this concept and help eliminate struggling unnecessarily.

LifeWorksInThrees.com